How To
Install Linux

by
Rick Bennette

ISBN-13: 978-1518625350
ISBN-10: 1518625355

Published by Beeline Publishing
Tequesta, Florida
www.beelinepublishing.com

Dedicated to Denise, the love of my life.

PREFACE

When your computer becomes sluggish and bogged down, it's probably the operating system. Windows is notorious for slowing down as time goes on. In addition, some versions of Windows are crash prone or hacked into quite easily. So why not change your operating system to one that is faster, more efficient and less likely to be hacked? If it's good enough for the Department of Defense, Google, IBM and many other Fortune 500 companies, no doubt you'll find it reliable and safe enough for your own needs.

This book will show you how to install Linux, and you don't need to be a technician to follow the simple step by step instructions. It's written for beginners. All it will cost you is one blank DVD. Linux and its apps are all free.

Linux can also be installed side by side with Windows, giving you the choice of running either operating system on your PC.

LINUX – IT OUTDOES WINDOWS

Here's the thing. Most everyday tasks don't really need the high speed of a new computer. Internet, word processing, music and photo editing, plus many more programs more will run fine on a ten year old computer, if that computer is running Linux as its operating system. With Linux, your computer will always work like new, maybe even better than new.

Advantages of Linux over Windows

Runs faster than Windows.
Uses less drive space than Windows.
Hardly ever crashes.
It's harder to hack than Windows.
Installs with no bloatware.
It's free.
It has thousands of free apps.
Runs on PC or Mac computers.
Runs on multiple computers.
No serial numbers.
Creates and reads files that are compatible with Windows programs.

Of course, Linux isn't perfect. You might find some of your programs won't work in Linux, but most Windows and Mac programs have Linux versions that are similar and create compatible files.

With most older PCs, whether laptop or desktop, the version of Windows Operating System (OS) that came with it might have been lost or become unavailable. Newer versions of Windows won't work on an old machine, because Windows is tied to the particular components within the machine it came with. For instance, the version of Windows that came with your machine was specifically mated to the video card, the motherboard, the sound card and all the other internal components. Your Windows disk isn't compatible with any other machine, and your machine isn't compatible with other versions of Windows unless specifically matched by the manufacturer.

You might get lucky and find an older version of Windows that loads into your machine, but maybe the sound card won't work or the monitor won't display properly. Or worse, it appears to work but then freezes up midway through a function. This happens because Windows is very particular in matching its software to the internal components of one specific PC. This was done intentionally so your version of Windows would only work on the one machine it came with.

If you have a Mac, there's a little more flexibility. The version of OS-10 that came with your machine might work on several other Macs of the same vintage. Still, some older Macs won't work properly with a newer version of OS-10.

Linux will install on almost any computer, whether it be a PC or Mac, a desktop or laptop. Linux is hardware independent, which means it has no trouble finding the hardware in your computer and matching it to its appropriate software drivers. Where Windows might require you to go on an internet hunting expedition to locate just the right software driver for each component in your computer, Linux will find them all by itself. I've never met a computer with which Linux would not work.

Linux, it should be known, is the operating

system used in all Android devices. It is also the core backbone of Google and most other major website servers. Why? Because Linux is simply by far the most reliable operating system on the planet. So why isn't it the major O.S. in all computers? Linux is an open source platform, and is not owned by any one company. It is designed and maintained by thousands of collaborators around the world.

AN EASY SOLUTION

This is going to sound so simple, you may not believe it when you read it. Linux is an Operating System that is so flexible and so efficient, that it almost defies logic how it can exist in a world where Windows is so finicky and expensive. The simple reason is Linux simply doesn't have the marketing power behind it that Apple or Microsoft have. Linux is so computer hardware independent, the same installation disk can be used on a both a PC or a Mac. You'll also be pleasantly surprised to know Linux is available as an online download at no cost.

Linux is totally cost-free and has no usage restrictions. You don't have to sign away your personal freedom and you don't have to suffer through any pop-up ads when you use it. In fact, it's so efficient, it can actually run faster on a ten year old machine than the original Windows or Mac OS that came with the machine. And Linux is much easier to install. You'll go through a few simple setup choices and then once you hit the Install button, the process requires no further input from you until it is installed.

Linux is an open source Operating System. Since many groups of designers have put their hands into designing Linux, it comes in a variety of versions. The version that looks and feels most like Windows or Mac OS10 is called Linux Mint. It is robust, it is stable, and best of all, a Linux computer is much more resistant from being hacked by outsiders than Windows or Mac.

Linux Mint is quite easy to learn for anyone familiar with Windows or Mac OS10. It runs pretty much all the same type of software as either Windows or Mac, only the 'buttons' are in slightly different places.

Linux comes pre-loaded with most of the commonly used applications, but with no bloatware or ads. Nothing pops up trying to automatically update your system unless you actively go in and ask for it.

Here's more good news. Although early versions of Linux were technical and hard for the average person to use, the latest versions are very close to Windows 7 and OS-10 in their appearance and function. Although not every software application made for Windows and Mac is available on Linux, most common apps are, albeit with different names. And all Linux apps are free.

If you've been using Microsoft Office for years, you'll be happy to know that even though MS Office isn't available on Linux, another program that looks and works just like Office is available. The files it creates are compatible between Linux, Mac and PC Operating systems. So the documents you made using MS Office in the past are usable on Linux, and the documents you create using the Linux based Libre Office program are compatible with MS Office programs on Macs and PCs. The same is true of

Powerpoint and Excel.

The photo below shows the Libre Office Writer program that comes free with Linux is quite similar to Microsoft Word.

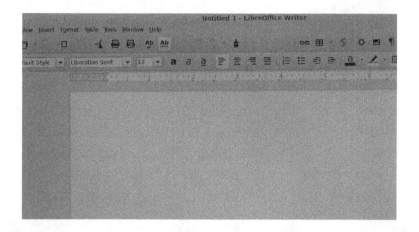

Most programs made for Windows or Mac have an equivalent similar program made for Linux. Photoshop, MS Word, Powerpoint, Excel, and many others all have similar Linux based programs available at no cost.

The only programs on Linux that I can't seem to find direct replacements for are the high end video editing programs like Final Cut Pro, Adobe Premier or Sony Vegas. Yes, Linux has several video editing programs, but they are not as robust.

WHY IS LINUX FREE?

Years ago, some of the software developers became disenchanted working for the major companies. These programmers set off on their own to create what they call open source software that anyone with enough technical skills could re-engineer and modify free of charge and free of copyright restriction. They created the Linux Operating system along with thousands of applications in order to give users a simple, reliable and free alternative to the established and expensive platforms.

You see, believe it or not, there are still quite a few programmers out there who love their work so much they're willing to do it and give it way for free, surviving only on the voluntary donations of about three hundred users worldwide. Income is secondary to seeing their work being used worldwide. Why? Who knows? These programmers have a different mindset than most business people, and money isn't what drives them. Thankfully for us, we get to reap the benefits.

TEST FIRST – INSTALL LATER

I do mention this in other places, but I want to bring it to your attention again because it's important.

You can run Linux directly off the DVD Install Disk without actually installing it onto your computer. This is called Test Mode, but it does everything the installed version does except save your settings when you exit.

Testing off the DVD allows you to try several different Linux versions before committing to a full install.

Since nothing is installed or saved on your hard drive in Test Mode, some users like to run their computers with Linux in Test Mode to do their online banking, because nothing is left behind after you remove the DVD.

Linux does run slower in Test Mode because it has to read all the instructions from the DVD directly, and that's a slower drive than a hard drive.

LET'S GET STARTED

To get started, you'll either need to have, or borrow, a working Windows or Mac computer connected to the internet. You'll also need a blank DVD disk (this is where your only cost comes in). The following instructions will show you how to download the proper Linux OS image file and burn it to a DVD.

Go to www.linuxmint.com. Keep in mind the web is a dynamic, ever changing place, so if in time that website changes, you can always Google 'Linux Mint' and find it again.

This is the home page of the Linux website, as of the publication date of this book. In the top menu, click 'Download'.

On the Download menu shown on the next page you'll see several choices under 'Download links'. The most common version and the one that most closely emulates Windows is named Cinnamon.

Selecting the 32 bit or 64 bit version of Linux is about the only choice you'll have to make in order to be sure Linux is compatible with your computer. All the other choices such as Cinnamon, Mate or Xfe are just different designs for how the desktop looks and feels. What's under the hood, so to speak, is pretty much the same in all versions of Linux.

If you aren't sure which type of machine you own, you can download and install both versions to see which one works. The 64 bit version should work in most machines. Install this version first. If the 64 bit doesn't work, then use the 32 bit version.

The latest default version is Linux Mint 17.2 Rafaela. You might be happy using this version.

Download Linux Mint 17.2 Rafaela

Information

Our latest release is Linux Mint 17.2, codename "Rafaela".

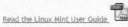
Read the Linux Mint User Guide

Read the release notes

Choose your favorite edition below. If you're not sure which one is right for you, "Cinnamon 64-bit edition" is the most popular.

Download links

EDITION				MULTIMEDIA SUPPORT *
Cinnamon	32-bit	64-bit	An edition featuring the Cinnamon desktop	Yes
Cinnamon No codecs	32-bit	64-bit	A version without multimedia support. For magazines, companies and distributors in the USA, Japan and countries where the legislation allows patents to apply to software and distribution of restricted technologies may require the acquisition of 3rd party licenses*.	No
Cinnamon OEM	64-bit		An installation image for manufacturers to pre-install Linux Mint.	No
MATE	32-bit	64-bit	An edition featuring the MATE desktop	Yes
MATE No codecs	32-bit	64-bit	A version without multimedia support. For magazines, companies and distributors in the USA, Japan and countries where the legislation allows patents to apply to software and distribution of	No

On my computer, I have found that 17.2 isn't quite as compatible as 17.0 Qiana. I had

13

some issues with 17.1 not working properly with my sound card. I continue to use Mint version 17.0 Qiana today. It is the most compatible and robust of all the Linux versions, and it works solidly without fail on all my PCs and Macs.

If you find you have problems with 17.2 Rafaela, alternatively, you can select the 'All Versions' link and download an older version like 17.0 Qiana, or for a really old machine, 13.0 Maya. All Linux versions are free, so experiment to see which one you like best.

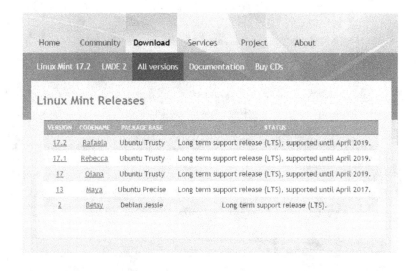

As you click to download, you'll see another menu for other versions including Mate.

These are basically the same program but with a different desktop. Try a few versions to see what you like best. Each file is about a gigabyte plus in size, so it'll take up to an hour each to download, depending upon your connection speed and the speed of the host.

EDITION	DESKTOP	MEDIA
Cinnamon (32-bit)	Cinnamon	DVD
Cinnamon (64-bit)	Cinnamon	DVD
Cinnamon no-codecs (32-bit)	Cinnamon	DVD
Cinnamon no-codecs (64-bit)	Cinnamon	DVD
Cinnamon OEM (64-bit)	Cinnamon	DVD
KDE (32-bit)	KDE	DVD
KDE (64-bit)	KDE	DVD
MATE (32-bit)	MATE	DVD
MATE (64-bit)	MATE	DVD
MATE no-codecs (32-bit)	MATE	DVD
MATE no-codecs (64-bit)	MATE	DVD
MATE OEM (64-bit)	MATE	DVD
Xfce (32-bit)	Xfce	DVD
Xfce (64-bit)	Xfce	DVD

Home   Community   **Download**   Services   Project   About

Linux Mint 17.2   LMDE 2   All versions   Documentation   Buy CDs

Editions for Linux Mint 17 "Qiana"

Next, you'll need to select one of the download sites. Choose one in the country of your residence. In the US, Linux Freedom or Metrocast seem to be the fastest. Of course,

15

this can change at any time, so experiment a bit.

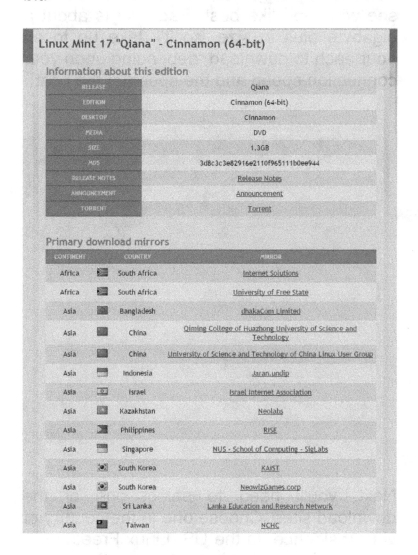

Linux Mint 17 "Qiana" - Cinnamon (64-bit)

Information about this edition

RELEASE	Qiana
EDITION	Cinnamon (64-bit)
DESKTOP	Cinnamon
MEDIA	DVD
SIZE	1.3GB
MD5	3d8c3c3e82916e2110f965111b0ee944
RELEASE NOTES	Release Notes
ANNOUNCEMENT	Announcement
TORRENT	Torrent

Primary download mirrors

CONTINENT	COUNTRY	MIRROR
Africa	South Africa	Internet Solutions
Africa	South Africa	University of Free State
Asia	Bangladesh	dhakaCom Limited
Asia	China	Qiming College of Huazhong University of Science and Technology
Asia	China	University of Science and Technology of China Linux User Group
Asia	Indonesia	Jaran.undip
Asia	Israel	Israel Internet Association
Asia	Kazakhstan	Neolabs
Asia	Philippines	RISE
Asia	Singapore	NUS - School of Computing - SigLabs
Asia	South Korea	KAIST
Asia	South Korea	NeowizGames corp
Asia	Sri Lanka	Lanka Education and Research Network
Asia	Taiwan	NCHC

16

The downloaded file is an ISO file, which is the type of file that creates your boot disk. This one file will contain everything you need to get started. It will create your boot disk, the Linux OS installer and several applications all onto one DVD-R disk.

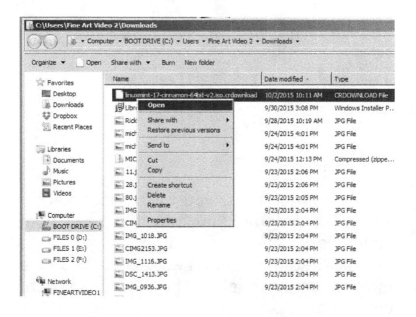

Once you have downloaded your completed ISO file, locate it in the download folder of your computer. This is most likely on your Boot drive.

Insert a blank DVD into your drive and double click on the ISO file. It should automatically bring up the Windows Disk Image Burner application that will begin to create your bootable Linux Install DVD.

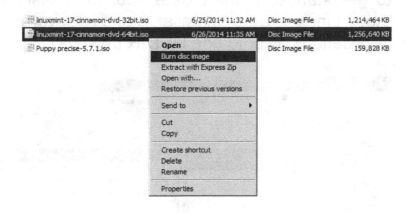

On some machines, you might be asked to select the program you want to use to burn your disk. This varies from machine to machine, so you might need to know a little more information about how your software creates a DVD.

Once you have successfully created the DVD, you're ready to begin the process of using the disk to test out Linux using this live DVD. Only after you test out Linux do you have to make a choice to install it permanently on a hard drive.

It is reassuring to know you can boot this disk and use it to test out Linux without erasing or destroying your current operating system, assuming the PC actually has a working operating system. You also won't disturb the files on your hard drive during the test phase. If you're not happy with using Linux, remove the disk, reboot your machine and it will work normally as it did before, assuming, of course, that it did work before. Otherwise, if it hasn't worked before, you have nothing at all to lose by installing Linux.

If you have multiple hard drives in your machine, you may wish to disconnect those drives that contain your saved files. This way, you won't make a mistake later on and select the wrong drive on which to install Linux.

All you need to do is power down your computer and remove the power plug from each unused hard drive. This prevents accidental erasure of those drives during the Linux installation. It is easy to misread the information and select the wrong drive.

You'll need to connect up your extra drives again after Linux is installed and working. Be sure to turn off the power to your PC before doing this.

Linux programs will be able to read most of the files currently on your drives, such as photos, music, videos, spreadsheets, etc. After all, what good would it be to create files on Linux if they weren't compatible with other users who have Windows PCs or Macs?

INSTALLING LINUX TEST MODE

You are less than an hour away from having your computer working like new. But first, there are a few things you might want to know about installing Linux.

The first thing you need to know is how your computer reads a DVD. When you boot your machine, it should read off the DVD first, then go to the hard drive to find the OS (Operating System). Most machines are set up to do this. But some older machines have to be manually changed to read the DVD first.

As you boot your machine, usually it will prompt you if you want to enter the BIOS (this is where you make the boot selection). Usually pressing the F2 or F10 key allows you to enter the BIOS.

Be careful here, because setting the BIOS improperly can prevent your computer from being able to boot up properly. It won't damage the hardware, but it can be frustrating to be locked out of booting your machine.

For Laptops Without A DVD Drive:

For netbooks and other computers without DVD drives, Linux can be installed from a USB flash drive 16 GIG or larger. Also, once installed on a USB flash drive, you can configure Linux to save any changes you make, unlike a read-only DVD-ROM drive. Here's how to install from a USB flash (or thumb) drive.

Insert a 16 Gig or larger flash drive into a USB port on your host computer. Using the Linux DVD you made on your host computer, install Linux onto the USB flash drive using the same procedure as you would to install to a hard drive. Just be sure you have selected the flash drive. When it's done, remove the flash drive from the host computer and insert it into a USB of your laptop.

Configure the BIOS in your laptop to boot first from a USB flash drive. With the USB drive already in the USB port of the laptop, boot your laptop. See the BIOS sample on the following page. Of course, your BIOS will be different than mine, but it should have a somewhat similar page to select the order of boot devices.

Your laptop will boot into Linux off the USB flash drive without affecting the current operating system that's on the hard drive.

Note: For Macs, you don't need to use the BIOS. Just hold down the Option key after the boot chime in order to boot from USB.

Try your version of Linux using the USB drive before installing it onto your hard drive. If you don't like using Linux on your laptop, simply remove the USB stick and reboot your laptop into its current operating system.

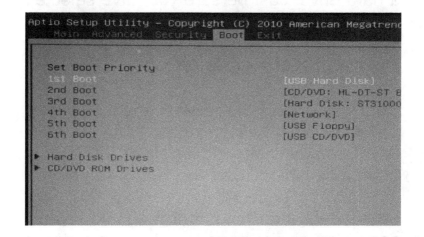

```
Set Boot Priority
1st Boot                              [USB Hard Disk]
2nd Boot                              [CD/DVD: HL-DT-ST E
3rd Boot                              [Hard Disk: ST31000
4th Boot                              [Network]
5th Boot                              [USB Floppy]
6th Boot                              [USB CD/DVD]

▶ Hard Disk Drives
▶ CD/DVD ROM Drives
```

You'll notice in the photo above, the BIOS is set to read the hard disk first. Set up this way, if your computer has a working operating system already on the hard drive, it means the Linux DVD won't be loaded in automatically simply by booting your computer. You'll have to change the boot order in the BIOS. This is easier than it sounds. The next photo shows a closeup of the BIOS set to read the DVD first. Set up like this, when you boot the computer, it will look at the DVD first, and if the disk has a valid OS install file, it will bring up that install process.

```
ght (C) 2010 American Megatrends, Inc.
 Boot  Exit


              [CD/DVD: HL-DT-ST B...]
              [Hard Disk: ST31000...]
              [USB Hard Disk]
              [Network]
              [USB Floppy]
              [USB CD/DVD]
```

Every BIOS is different, so I can't tell you the exact method your machine uses, aside from the most likely methods I've already provided. If you need help changing your boot menu, I'm sure you can find a friend, relative or colleague who will be able to assist you..

Automatic boot in 4 seconds...

OK, let's assume you can now boot off the DVD drive. The Linux DVD you have just created is a live DVD. It bears repeating that this disk is capable of booting the machine and being usable as an Operating System (OS) without disturbing or erasing anything on your hard drive. This means you can test out your machine with Linux, without messing up the OS already on your computer, providing it already has one.

Linux will run slowly in the test mode, because almost every command you input has to access the DVD drive. Remember, the entire Linux operating system is running off the disk along with the RAM memory in your computer, but it is not using the hard drive. Using your computer in the test mode is a relatively slow process compared with accessing the O.S. off the hard drive. But don't worry. It's only this slow in the test mode.

Once in the test mode, the Linux home screen comes up appearing as if no additional software is installed. Don't worry. There are many usable programs you can try out in the test mode. You just need to access the spot where the programs are located and copy their icons to your desktop. There's no bloatware or ads in Linux, so your desktop is bare until you put something there.

You have two choices at this point. You can create a mock setup of your desktop to see how it will look, and then test out some of the apps without committing to a real install. Whatever you set up on the desktop is not saved in test mode, so you may not want to spend much time setting up your system until you have installed Linux on your hard drive. To access the apps, click on 'Menu' at the lower left corner of the screen.

Navigate the menu items on the middle column using the left click, then from the right column, right click an app and click on 'Add to Desktop' to create a desktop icon for that app.

After playing around a bit and discovering what some of the apps do, If you are satisfied Linux will work, (it will if the test mode comes up OK) you can begin the process of installing Linux on your hard drive.

As mentioned before, it is a good idea to disconnect any hard drives that are not going to be used for the installation. Laptops usually don't give this choice because they only have one hard drive.

If you decide Linux isn't for you, or you want to try another version, or perhaps you want to go back to Windows (Why? I don't know), then simply reboot the machine and remove the disk.

To try another version of Linux, create and insert another Install disk with a different Linux version using the methods already outlined in this book. This way, you can try out several versions to see which you like best, and which works best with your sound card, screen, etc.

Installing Linux erases the entire drive, so if you have files you need to save, and if you can access them, save them on another medium before permanently installing Linux to your hard drive.

Use DVD disks, thumb drives or an external hard drive to save your files, assuming this PC works. If not, you may wish to remove the hard drive, connect it to another machine and save the files you need before remounting the hard drive for your Linux install.

INSTALLING LINUX TO
THE HARD DRIVE

Linux works best when running off a hard drive, but it is also possible to install Linux to, and run it off, a USB thumb drive (as long as the thumb drive capacity is large enough).

When you are ready to begin the permanent install process, double click the 'Install Linux Mint' icon and give it time to read the disk. The reboot process will begin and will take some time.

Once Linux Install is loaded, you'll see the screen above. Select your language, give it a second, and hit 'Continue'.

The next screen will ask you to enter your internet connection information if you are using a wireless connection.

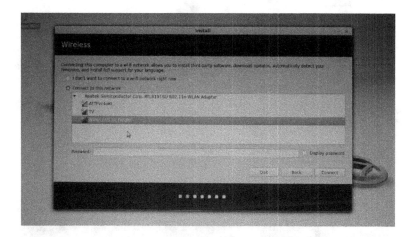

Choose your wireless connection and enter your password.

If you are wired in to the internet, you will only see a message that tells you you are connected to the internet, but no password request.

When you are ready, click 'Continue'.

You will then see a resource screen advising the amount of blank space you'll need on your drive, and that you are connected to the internet.

If it's a laptop, you'll also see a message advising you to connect to a power source as opposed to using the battery power. It's a good idea to use AC power if you can.

Click 'Continue'.

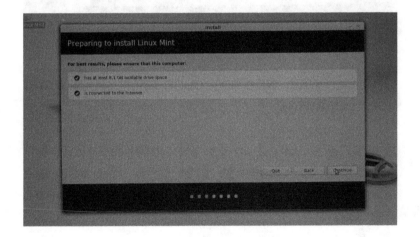

The next screen asks if you want a full install or an install alongside of the existing OS (in this example, Linux Qiana).

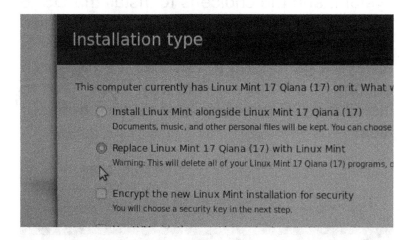

It is advisable to completely replace the OS with a fresh installation. Linux boots up faster this way. Of course, if Windows still works on your computer and you want to use it on occasion, you have the option of using either operating system. It'll just be an extra manual input choice to make during the boot up process.

You can choose to encrypt you installation, but this makes Linux run slower.

Make your choices and press 'Continue'.

On the next screen, you'll be able to select the hard drive where Linux will install. In the example, there are three drives in the system, and the choice is to install the OS to the smallest 'C' drive, leaving the other two larger drives to hold the files. In practice, it is always a good idea to have all the files on a second or third drive. This way, if you need to install the OS again, you don't wipe out your files.

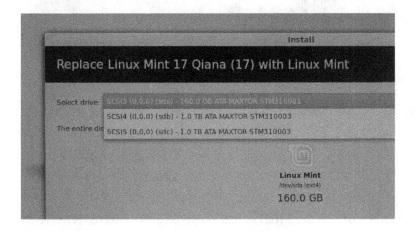

Worthy of mentioning again is this. You can choose to install Linux to a thumb drive if that drive has enough capacity. This is a good choice if you'd like to move Linux from machine to machine and use it without disturbing the existing operating system on the machine. Removing the thumb drive takes the operating system with you. The advantage of a thumb drive over using the DVD test mode is that your desk top and any files you put on the thumb drive are saved and can travel with you.

Some people like to use this method to keep their banking files off the computer itself. Naturally this is safe from the perspective of not having the next user see your data after removing the thumb drive, but you'll want to them make sure that thumb drive isn't misplaced or lost.

When you are satisfied you've made the right choice in drives, double click the 'Install Now' button. This is your final opportunity to check to see you aren't going to erase the wrong drive.

The next screen lets you pick your time zone.

Next, select your keyboard language.

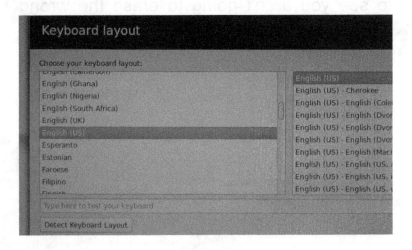

On the next screen. enter your name, password and computer name. This is the only personal information you will be asked to enter.

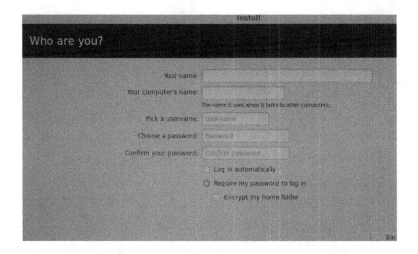

You must enter a password, but you can choose whether you want the computer to boot up without needing your password.

Once you press the 'Continue' button, the installation process will begin. You won't have to make any more selections. It takes between ten and sixty minutes to install, depending upon your processor and hard drive speed. It is a little slower installing to a thumb drive than a hard drive.

When the process is completed, it will ask you if you want to continue retesting or restart. You might need to restart a second time after removing the install disk.

The home screen will look like it did in the test mode except the install icon will not be shown as it is here. Since the computer is now running Linux off the hard drive, it will work much faster than id did when it was running in the test mode. Additionally, any changes you make to your desktop setup, and any of your newly made files will now be saved on your hard drive.

The basic Linux setup is now completed, and it's time to add your icons and additional programs from the Linux web site, should you desire to do so.

ADDING SOFTWARE and USING LINUX

This isn't a comprehensive instruction book for using all of the features of Linux, but you should know a few basics to get you started.

In the lower left hand corner Click on 'Menu'. A sub-menu comes up with all the applications that are included on the install disk. Navigate the menu items in the **middle** column using the **left** click mouse button.

From the **right** column, **right** click an app. Click 'Add to Desktop' to create a desktop icon for that app.

If this is your first time using Linux, your probably saying to yourself, "I have no idea what these programs are."

Once you load in some apps, your screen will look like this.

Click on 'All Applications' to see the complete list on the right. Use the scroll bar to see all hundred or so apps. Some are self explanatory, and some you'll wonder what they do. Here are some hints for the common apps and the apps they are equivalent to in Windows.

Gimp Image Editor is a close clone of Photoshop. (shown above)

Firefox is your web browser.

Brasero is a CD and DVD maker. This is what you will use to burn your music, data and video disks.

Banshee is a video and media player that will play almost any video and audio file.

Libre Office Draw is a paint program.

Libre Office Calc is a spreadsheet like MS

Excel.

Libre Office Impress is like MS Powerpoint.

Libre Office Writer is like MS Word. As you can see in the following screen shot, it looks similar in its menu structure. If you want to save files for use in MS Word, you'll do a 'Save As' function and select the Doc extension. You may need to perform a similar typr of 'Save As' command in other programs as well, if you want your files to be compatible with other programs outside of Linux.

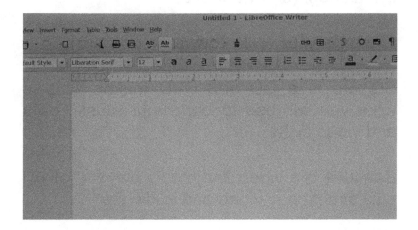

There are thousands of other free apps that are not included on the install disk, but are available online at no cost. You can access these apps by double clicking on the included app called 'Software Manager'. This accesses the internet and provides a search bar to get you closer to what you need.

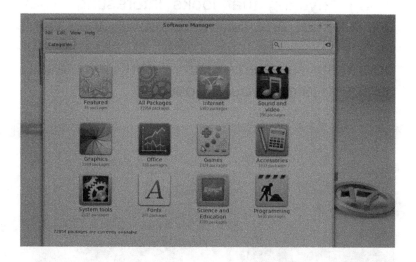

Audacity is a great audio editing program. You can add this to those already provided on the install disk. Simply type audacity into the search bar at the top right.

Kino is a video capture and basic editing program. You can type Kino in the search bar to find it.

By clicking on one of the large icons, you can find apps related to that main category.

You'll find that many of the apps are rated by users. The higher rated apps are naturally the most revered, and likely the best in their category. But that shouldn't stop you from trying anything that looks interesting. They are all free, and unlike Windows, they don't bury themselves into unseen corners of your operating system. They can be easily removed later if you choose.

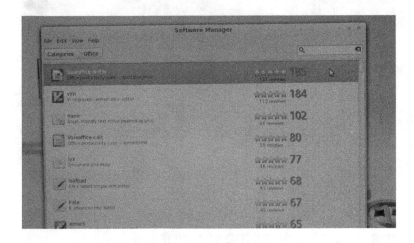

If I were to continue, this book would be hundreds of pages long simply describing the thousands of apps. I'll leave the rest to you to discover on your own.

There is a system Setting menu to customize the operation of Linux. Those of you with previous Mac experience may notice the familiarity of the Linux 'Systems Setting' screen.

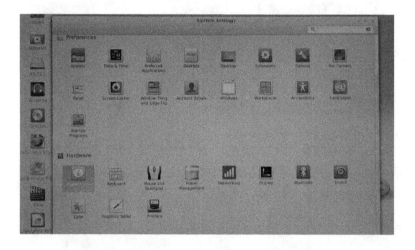

Folders and files may be stored and located using what looks like 'My Computer' on a Windows machine. You can see the similarities of these and many other parts of Linux as you poke around and experiment. You'll find new names for programs you are likely to be already familiar with by a different name.

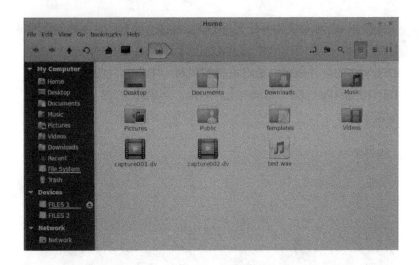

Of course, if you need to know what resources are inside your computer, you can access the 'System Settings' screen.

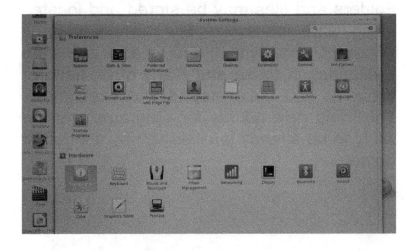

Feel free to experiment. Click on each of the many buttons to see what each one does. Most are quite self explanatory.

Enjoy the use of your computer with its new operating system. If you like the way Linux works, please pass the word about this instructional manual on to your friends.

MORE BOOKS

For more books by this author,
please search
Rick Bennette at Amazon.com

Just Plane Gone
Take My Heart
My Little Angel
Expectations
Infidelity
Tough Love
Aliens In Paradise
Last Chance
Two Suns
Moon Boys

www.ingramcontent.com/pod-product-compliance
Lightning Source LLC
Chambersburg PA
CBHW061036050326
40689CB00012B/2853